HIDDEN SUSPECT

HIDDEN SUSPECT

Jeremy Brown

CRIME FILE INVESTIGATIONS

SCHOLASTIC

Scholastic Children's Books,
Euston House, 24 Eversholt Street,
London NW1 1DB, UK

A division of Scholastic Ltd
London ~ New York ~ Toronto ~ Sydney ~ Auckland
Mexico City ~ New Delhi ~ Hong Kong

First published in the US by Scholastic Inc
as the second half of *Body of Evidence*, 2005
First published in the UK by Scholastic Ltd, 2006

Text copyright © Jeremy Brown, 2005

10 digit ISBN 0 439 95012 0
13 digit ISBN 978 0439 95012 1

Printed and bound by Nørhaven Paperback A/S, Denmark

2 4 6 8 10 9 7 5 3 1

Contents

PERSONNEL FILE

CSI Wes Burton

Burton is a witty, intelligent investigator who loves the problem-solving nature of crime scene investigation. His signature fly-fisherman's waistcoat, bristling with evidence-gathering tools, is a welcome sight at any crime scene (except those run by Detective Gibson). Not much surprises Burton, including a criminal's ability to weave a nearly perfect lie. He usually prefers evidence analysis to talking to witnesses and suspects because, unlike people, "evidence stands up; it does not lie." He appreciates Detective Radley's interviewing skills and her interest in why a crime occurred, because it allows him to focus on the how.

Detective Erin Radley

At six-foot-one, Detective Radley can be an intimidating woman. Her motto, "Convict them with kindness", seems in conflict with her physical appearance, but it is that contradiction that keeps suspects off balance and talking to her. When a woman of her stature hands you a blanket and hot chocolate, then asks why you stabbed your wife, it's hard to concentrate on your lie. Radley has a master's degree in psychology and tends to focus on the why of a case. She plans to publish a study one day on what compels criminals to commit their crimes. Working with Burton presents plenty of odd situations that will help her book stand out. She appreciates Burton's dedication to solving crimes and his ability to lighten situations that most individuals would find disturbing and depressing.

Detective Frank Gibson

Gibson is what he would call "old school", using intimidation and a loud voice to get a confession rather than patience and by-the-book techniques. In some cases his approach is required, such as when a kidnapper won't divulge the location of his latest victim, but for the most part Burton and his team do not appreciate Gibson's presence at a crime scene. Gibson and Burton constantly clash with each other, and when it comes to solving a crime, they have an unspoken competition to see who can identify the perpetrator first. The perpetrators don't stand a chance.

Mike Trellis

Trellis is Burton's CSI technician assistant. He specializes in trace analysis, arson and horrible jokes, such as commenting that a shooting victim died from "Too much lead in his diet." It doesn't help that he follows every joke with "Get it?" Burton knows that when Trellis is working on a case, he can expect close attention to detail, exhaustive analysis of evidence and dedication to finding the guilty party. Detective Gibson likes to pick on Trellis, but the young technician has a knack for frustrating the burly cop, and for that, Burton likes him even more.

Lauren Crown

Dr Crown is a shy, almost reclusive forensic pathologist. A genius in her field, she is nearly incapable of having a normal conversation. However, she is quick to recite the qualifications of a forensic pathologist should anyone refer to her as a medical examiner, or worse, a coroner. She can determine a corpse's time of death within ten minutes just by looking at it, but she has no idea who the president of the United States is – and doesn't care.

Ed

Ed, short for Exhibit D, is a search-and-rescue border collie. She was adopted and trained by Burton after being admitted as evidence in a case against her owner, a methamphetamine dealer. Her fur contained trace elements of the ingredients used to make the drug, and the dealer was convicted. She can follow ground and air scent and is in training to become a certified cadaver dog as well.

Burian U Gorlach

Burian, or Bug, as he prefers to be called, is a Russian immigrant and the owner of Sensitive

Cleaners, a company that cleans and decontaminates crime scenes when an investigation is complete. Bug is anything but sensitive, muttering in semi-English and cackling while he rips up bloodstained carpets and vacuums biohazards.

BRINGING THE TRUTH TO LIGHT

"Boy, this guy's a worse driver than my wife," Detective Gibson said, standing next to the wrecked truck on the side of the road. "And she's half blind."

"That explains why she married you," said Burton as he tied off the end of his CRIME SCENE – DO NOT CROSS/CRIME SEEN? STICK AROUND tape. Mike Trellis coughed to hide his smile. It was nearly 9.00 pm and the sky was dark, but the portable lights and road flares bathed the scene as if it were day.

"Why don't you quickly crawl under the front tyre, Burton," Gibson said. "I want to check something."

"What?" Burton asked, peering around the tyre in question.

"How long you can live with the front tyre on top of you," Gibson replied.

"Aw, there's that police brotherhood thing I've been hearing about," Trellis said. "It brings a tear to my eye."

"All right, boys," Burton said. "Let's get down to business. Gibson, do you have the driver's statement?"

Gibson flipped open his notepad. "The driver, Glenn Ward, was driving down St Joseph Avenue, the road we are currently standing on, around 8.00 pm He didn't have his headlights on and didn't see the joggers until it was too late. His vehicle struck all four joggers, killing two of them, putting one in critical condition. They all had reflective vests on, but it didn't matter since his lights were off. They're at Lakeview Hospital right now. Ward got a sprained ankle and a bloody nose, treated and released by the Emergency Medical Technicians. He's in the back of that squad car right now." Gibson pointed to a police car across the road, about 50 yards away. "He's pretty upset over the whole thing, and he keeps saying 'I told them, I told them.'"

"Told who what?" Burton asked.

"Let's go and see," Gibson said, and headed for the squad car.

"Mr Ward, this is Wes Burton, he's a crime scene investigator," said Gibson. Ward looked up from the passenger seat. He held a bloody paper towel under his nose.

"Hello," he said and checked the towel for fresh blood. Apparently satisfied, he let his hands fall into his lap.

"Earlier you were saying 'I told them.' Can you explain what that meant?" Gibson asked.

"Yeah," Ward said. "I see those joggers just about every night on my way home from work, and the other day I pulled over and talked to them. They run in the road, all spread out alongside each other, instead of single file on the path like they should. I told them that I had to swerve into oncoming traffic to avoid them, and it made me nervous."

"And tonight you just didn't see them?" Gibson said.

"Right," said Ward. "I didn't think it was dark enough for my headlights. I guess they didn't see me coming, and I sure didn't see them. They shouldn't have been in the road like that anyway, right?"

"Thanks, Mr Ward," Burton said. "Just wait here, please." Burton and Gibson walked back to the truck, where Trellis was shining a torch into the broken right headlight.

"Check it out, boss," he said. Burton took the torch and peered into the broken headlight. After a few moments, he took his portable inspection microscope out of waistcoat pocket 20 and focused it through the jagged glass. The small tool could magnify items from 18 up to 36 times.

"What are you looking at?" Gibson said.

"The wire inside the headlight," said Burton, still peering through his mini microscope.

"You mean the filament?" Gibson said, and Burton looked at him with raised eyebrows.

"Well, yes," he said, "but I didn't think you'd know what that word meant."

"Please," said Gibson. "I do all the work on my Chevys myself. I can swap out a starter and change the oil in the time it takes Trellis here to comb his hair."

Trellis touched his head. "Is my hair OK?"

Gibson ignored him. "Why are you looking at the filament?" he said to Burton.

"As you know," Burton said, thinking he'd never say those words to Gibson, "the filament in a headlight is a thin wire encased in a tube of glass. When electricity is passed through the wire, it becomes extremely hot and creates a bright beam of light."

"I'm still with you," Gibson said.

"When Ward hit the joggers," said Burton, "it broke the tube of glass around the filament, but the filament stayed intact. Take a close look at the filament and tell me what you see."

Trellis stepped forwards, and Burton held his hand up. "I was talking to Gibson," he said. The technician's mouth opened then closed. Gibson smiled at him then examined the filament through the mini microscope.

"I see little beads of glass on the filament," Gibson said. "But I've gotta tell you, I don't know what significance that has."

Trellis finally got his mouth to work. "Maybe if I had a look, it would jog my memory. Get it? Because they were jogging."

"I changed my mind," Gibson said. "I want you to get under the tyre instead of Burton." He turned to the head CSI. "So what is it about the filament? What did you see?"

"I saw evidence that needs some running shoes of its own, because it'll be standing up in court," Burton said. "Ward saw the joggers coming, and he hit them on purpose."

How did he know?

Burton's File

When the headlight broke, pieces of glass came in contact with the filament and melted, forming the beads. For this to happen, the filament had to have been extremely hot, indicating that Ward had his headlights on when he hit the joggers.

DENTAL BREAKDOWN

Burton and Detective Gibson stood next to the hospital bed and looked down at Rick Willard, who was in a coma. Willard's entire body was swollen, but his legs, ankles and feet were especially puffy. Bruises covered most of his arms, and there were a few splotches on his face and neck where it looked like he'd taken a few punches.

"He's got it right," Burton said. "If you have to be in a hospital, you're best off being in a coma. That way, you don't even know you're there." Burton didn't like hospitals one bit.

"Maybe he does know," Gibson said. "I mean, the poor guy's in a coma from his kidneys failing after he takes a beating, and you're here talking about how lucky he is. I think he'd rather be awake and watching bad daytime TV and eating junk food. Maybe he can hear you right now, and he's adding you to the list of people he's going to chase when he wakes up." He looked at Willard. "Mr Willard, Detective Gibson. I think you look great, and I] you get better really soon." He smiled at Burt happy that he wasn't on Willard's hit list.

"Can I take my samples and go?" Burton asked.

"Who's stopping you?" Gibson said, stepping back from the bed. Burton gently lifted Willard's left hand and looked at the fingernails. There was nothing there. He did the same with the right hand and again found nothing.

"There's no trace evidence under the fingernails," Burton said. "I don't think he put up much of a fight when he was attacked."

"There wasn't any sign of a struggle at his home," Gibson said. "I talked to the guy who lives next door, and he didn't hear anything that sounded like a fight. It's possible that whoever did this beat him up somewhere else, and he made it home before passing out. And I tell you, for a dentist, it wasn't that nice a place."

"Willard is a dentist?" said Burton, opening his pad to take down the new information.

"I assume so," Gibson said. "His apartment had that smell."

"What smell?" Burton didn't start writing.

"You know, that dentist smell. They all have it."

"Do you mean dentists' surgeries have the smell, or the dentists do?" Burton asked.

"What?"

"Did you smell something in his apartment that reminded you of a dentist's surgery," Burton said slowly, "or of your dentist in particular?"

d for a moment. "The dentist's ⌐cided. "I don't know what my

⌐him and lifted the medical chart ⌐the bed. He glanced down the face ⌐he came to the line "Occupation." ⌐ard is unemployed," he said.

⌐h," said Gibson. "Then I guess his apartment was pretty nice."

"He wouldn't have been likely to have been in a dentist's surgery as a patient, let alone as the dentist. So where did that smell come from?"

"Not from me," Gibson said. "I had chilli for lunch. If it came from me, it wouldn't smell like a dentist's."

Burton flipped through the chart some more. "The doctor checked his mouth for broken or missing teeth and found extreme swelling and inflammation along the upper gum line, but it had been there for a few days, so it wasn't a result of the fight. So Willard had a toothache but couldn't go to the dentist."

"So he had a dentist come to him?" Gibson offered. "And when he couldn't pay, the dentist beat him up? We've got a slimy, vicious dentist on the loose!"

"I don't think so," Burton said. "The culprit we're looking for is oily, and it's still in Willard's apartment."

How did he know?

Willard had a terrible toothache and used clove oil to soothe the pain. Eugenol, the active ingredient in clove oil, was the source of the "dentist smell." It's used as a pain reliever by dental professionals and is in most over-the-counter toothache medicines. What Willard didn't know is that an overdose of clove oil can cause kidney failure, which can result in swelling, bruising and, eventually, coma.

DOUGHNUT ASSUME

Burton parked his truck and walked towards the small doughnut shop. What was left of it, anyway.

"Watch the glass," Detective Radley said from inside the burnt-out building. The street was peppered with shards of glass, which flew as far as 40 feet when the doughnut shop exploded.

"Good thing this happened at night, when no one was around," Burton said. "We'd have some people puzzles to put back together."

Mike Trellis was collecting sample materials from inside the shop and placing them in sealed glass jars. He was working quickly, because if the explosion was the result of arson and the criminal used an accelerant such as petrol, the trace vapours would soon evaporate.

"Can you imagine the jokes we're going to get about this?" Trellis asked. "People will say that the cops will solve this one in a hurry, as it was a doughnut shop."

"I don't buy doughnuts," Burton said. "I'm a muffin guy."

"Really?" Trellis stopped his collection process and looked suspiciously at Burton. "How come?"

"You get more for your money with a muffin," Burton said. "A doughnut comes with a hole in it. It's a matter of economics, really."

Radley nodded at this, seeing the logic.

"What about doughnuts with filling?" Trellis asked, sounding like he hoped he'd ruined Burton's theory with one question.

"Those are for suckers," Burton replied, and Trellis sagged. "It's like they're saying, 'We know we're ripping you off by having a hole in the middle, so here's some jam to keep you quiet.' No thanks. Not for me."

"Interesting," Radley said, more to herself than the two crime-scene investigators. "I wonder if a person's choice of breakfast pastry is an indicator of any other behaviour in his or her life... Maybe this could be a sub-chapter in my book."

"But I've seen you eat doughnuts before," Trellis said, a look of complete confusion on his face.

"Oh, I'll eat doughnuts," Burton said. "I just won't buy them."

Trellis shook his head. "I think your doughnut theory has a few holes in it," he said. "Get it? Because of—"

"Yeah, I get it," Burton interrupted. Then he asked, "What do you think happened here?"

"From the spread of the glass and destruction of the kitchen in the back," Trellis said, resuming his sample taking, "it was definitely an explosion. Whether it was gas or placed explosives, I'm not sure yet. I've found a few melted kitchen timers that could have been used as part of an explosive device, but it's a doughnut shop, so they might just be ordinary old timers."

"Is the owner looking at a big insurance payoff after this?" Burton asked Radley.

"He is insured, but it's not a huge amount by any means," she said. "And he's not struggling, either. This shop does very well during the week, and there's a queue out of the door most weekends."

"He makes a great New York cheesecake doughnut," Trellis said, then gave Burton a flat look. "Not that you'd know."

Burton rolled his eyes at Radley. "I'll check out the back," he said. "See if there are any tyre marks from someone making a quick getaway."

Behind the doughnut shop, Burton found stacks of plastic crates, a rubbish bin, a recycling bin and several parking places – but no fresh tyre marks. He checked the rear security door to the shop and saw no signs of forced entry, then he headed for the rubbish bin. He was constantly amazed at what criminals threw away, as if the rubbish bin were some portal to another dimension instead of a handy holding tank for clues.

Burton took one look in the rubbish bin, smiled, and went to get Radley and Trellis. When he brought them back, they didn't share his happiness.

"Eggs?" Radley said. "Why would he throw out dozens of eggs?"

Trellis leaned into the bin and inhaled deeply. Radley shuddered. "They don't smell rotten," he said.

"They aren't," Burton said. "But the doughnut maker thought they were. You can dunk the arson investigation. This was an accident."

How did Burton know?

Gas which is used for cooking and heating, is invisible and odourless. In order for us to detect possible leaks, Mercaptan, which contains sulphur, is added to the gas. If you've ever smelled sulphur before, you won't forget it. It smells like rotten eggs.

The gas leak in the doughnut bakery made the chef think his eggs were rotten, so he threw them away.

EXIT, STAGE DEATH

"This is Rufus Weatherton, the stage manager here at the Civic Theatre," Detective Radley said, introducing Burton and Mike Trellis.

"Pleased to make your acquaintance," Weatherton said, his English accent sounding very impressive. The four of them stood on the theatre's stage, near the front. They were careful to stay out of the crime scene, near centre stage, in the middle of scenery that hadn't been touched since the night before.

"Likewise," said Burton. "Although you're probably wishing that we could meet under different circumstances."

"Dreadful situation, isn't it?" Weatherton said. "As far as I know, the Civic has never before had an actor die in the middle of a performance. And on opening night! We've had a few stagehands pass on during shows, the drunken sots. They fall from the catwalks like they get paid extra to do so!"

"Maybe they should call them 'can't walks' instead," Trellis offered. "Get it? Because they're hard to walk on." Weatherton looked at Trellis as though he were a Martian. Burton coughed.

"So," Radley said to Weatherton as she shot Trellis a harsh look. "The performer's name was Shelly Victoria, and she died of unknown causes during Act Two, is that correct?"

"Indeed," Weatherton said. "It was during the only dance number in the production, Miss Victoria's tap routine. The director added it in at the last moment, though none of us could understand why."

"Did the director and Victoria have any trouble?" Radley asked.

"Oh, they despised one another," Weatherton said huffily. "They used to be a lovey couple before the production, but there were some arguments during rehearsals, and eventually they could barely stand to be in the same room. Even when the room's this big." He gestured towards the theatre's cathedral ceiling.

"And she just dropped to the stage?" Burton asked.

"I'm afraid so," said Weatherton. "My guess would be a heart attack or stroke, except she was so young."

"Her medical records didn't show a history of heart trouble or high cholesterol," Burton said. "But rest assured, our forensic pathologist, Dr Crown, will be able to determine the cause of death," Burton said. "But while we wait, let's see if we can figure it out ourselves. Thanks for your time, Mr Weatherton."

"If you need anything at all," Weatherton said with a small bow, "I'll be right over here." He walked offstage, where he checked his hair in a mirror.

"Did he go stage left or stage right?" Trellis asked. "I can never remember."

"It's your left and right as you stand onstage and face the audience," Burton said, turning to look at the empty seats.

"Does the audience call it 'audience left'?" Trellis asked.

"Mike – check the crime scene," Burton said. Once he was busy, Radley leaned towards Burton.

"This is a tremendous opportunity," she said in a low voice.

"You want to get into acting?" Burton asked, surprised.

"No, for my book," said Radley. "Criminals are liars, and who knows more about lying than an actor? They're professional liars! I could get some great insight into motivation, techniques for altering one's personality and—"

Radley stopped short when she saw Weatherton standing next to her. She hoped he hadn't heard the part about professional liars. He had. Weatherton looked around to make sure no one else was within earshot before he spoke.

"It's true, in the theatre, we lie," Weatherton said, and the twangy southern accent that came out of his mouth made Burton do a double take.

"My name isn't Weatherton, it's Boyd," he said. "I figure y'all should hear it from me instead of someone else, or it might seem like I'm hiding my identity."

"Thanks, Mr Boyd," Radley said, still thrown off by the accent. "Is there anything else we should know?"

"Not about me," Boyd said. "Except that I didn't kill Victoria. She was a stage manager's dream. We had the first week sold out before opening night because of her. She worked hard and never complained. Except about the director, of course. She wanted to have him fired from day one. I think he put that dance number in the show just to get back at her. Can you imagine? Making the leading lady tap-dance in a puddle! In a scene that takes place in the desert!"

"Thanks again, Mr Boyd," Burton said, and left him with Radley. He headed over to Trellis, who was following an extension lead from backstage, through the scenery, to where it ended at centre stage.

"What did you find?" Burton asked.

"This lead is plugged in over there, runs hidden through the set and ends here," Trellis said. "But there's no plug on this end. It's just frayed wires."

"Detective Radley," Burton called. "We need to send some officers to arrest the director. I want to talk to him about his electrifying opening night."

How did Victoria die?

Burton's File

The director was upset about his breakup with Shelly Victoria and wanted to end her career – for good. He put in the last-minute scene that had her tap-dance in a puddle, then added a prop of his own – the frayed extension lead. When she stepped into the puddle, the electricity from the lead flowed into the metal taps on her shoes, electrocuting Victoria.

FIRST-DEGREE BIRDER

Ed leaped over logs and scuttled under branches, hot on the trail, her orange vest jingling with every step. Burton followed, not quite out of breath but wishing he had Ed's stamina. They were in the forest, with hundreds of square miles of woods, valleys, hills and fields to search.

"Good girl, Ed, keep going," Burton said. Almost before he could finish the sentence, Ed bounded back towards him and sat down, her ears up and her body leaning ahead, anxious to lead Burton to the source of the scent.

"What did you find? Show me!" Burton said, breaking into a sprint. Ed took off, leading Burton to a stand of pine trees that formed a canopy. Ed disappeared into the spiny branches, and Burton heard a voice say "Good girl! What a smarty!"

Ed emerged from the trees, followed by Mike Trellis, the subject of the search. He and Burton were working Ed through some search-and-rescue drills to keep her sharp and happy. She was a working dog and didn't enjoy unemployment.

"Good job, Exhibit D!" Burton said and tossed her a tennis ball. The ball was Ed's reward for a job well done, and she had been expecting the throw with wide eyes and a blurred tail.

"Did she have any trouble finding me?" Trellis asked, brushing pine needles off his clothes.

"Not really," Burton said. "A few hitches when she found some raccoon poop, but no big problems. It probably helped that you had burritos for dinner last night. She probably thought she was tracking a septic tank."

"Help!"

Trellis closed his mouth before he could respond to Burton's jab. "Did you hear that?" he asked instead.

"Sounded like 'help,' " Burton answered, his head tilted to the side.

"Someone help!" The voice sounded close by, but Burton knew the acoustics in this kind of terrain were tricky. He could tell which direction it was coming from, though, and he and Trellis started that way.

"Come on, Ed," Burton said. "Bring your ball." Ed trotted along with the two men, her ball held loosely in her mouth. The three of them travelled for about ten minutes, using a call-and-response system with the voice to home in on the caller's location. Finally, they came to a small clearing, where a man stood over a figure lying face up in the dirt.

"Thank goodness!" the man said, his voice hoarse from all the shouting. "I think this guy might be in trouble. I don't think he's breathing!"

Trellis knelt by the prone man and listened for breathing, then checked for a pulse. Nothing. When his fingers left the man's throat, the white spots caused by their pressure quickly returned to the man's normal skin tone.

"I'm going to initiate CPR," Trellis said and opened the man's jacket, which had the *Field Guide to North American Birds* sticking out of a front pocket. Poking out from another pouch was a tattered notebook, and a small pair of binoculars lay on the ground next to the man's foot.

Once he was sure Trellis didn't need assistance, Burton looked at the man who called for help, who was now sitting on a log with his head in his hands. He noticed a similar spotting scope around his neck and a patch on his jacket that said "the kirtland's warbler club – membership: 1"

"Are you two bird-watchers?" Burton asked.

"Birders," the man said without looking up.

"Birders?" said Burton. "So you bird?"

"That's right. What's the problem?"

"Well," Burton said. "Runners run, climbers climb, so birders ... bird?"

"No, we spot birds and record the sightings," the man said, finally looking at Burton. "Who are you, anyway? I've been shouting for over an hour."

"I'm Wes Burton, CSI and this is Mike Trellis, my technician. That's Ed, my dog. And your name is?"

"Eagle Eye Dorchester," the man said. Burton

looked at him. "Thomas Dorchester," he said after a moment.

"OK, Thomas," Burton said. "What happened here?"

"I was in a great spot," Dorchester said, "trying to attract a black-backed woodpecker, when I heard this yelp and a crash, like branches breaking. I ran over here to see what happened and found him like this. I didn't even know he was out here until then. I think he fell out of a tree."

Burton looked at Trellis, who had given up on the CPR and was checking for signs of trauma. "There's blood on the back of his head," Trellis said. "Could be a fractured skull, caused by a blow to the head. Or a fall, I suppose."

"Do you know this man's name?" Burton asked Dorchester.

"No, I've never seen him out here before," he said.

Burton slipped on a latex glove from waistcoat pocket 5 and eased the tattered notebook out of the man's pouch. He flipped through the pages, hoping to find an If found, please return to So-and-So notice. The pages were filled with sketches and scribblings of birds spotted, and the entry on the last written page caught Burton's eye. It was written in large block letters, surrounded by exclamation points: "THE KIRTLAND'S WARBLER! Perched on branch and singing!"

"That's a pretty exclusive club you're in," Burton said, pointing to Dorchester's patch. "Did you know that everyone in it is a murderer?"

How did Burton know?

Dorchester said that he'd been shouting for help for over an hour, but when Trellis checked the body for a pulse, his fingers made white marks on the tissue. When he removed the pressure, blood flowed back into the tissue, returning it to its normal colour. This is called blanching and only occurs when a body has been dead for less than 30 minutes. When Trellis, Ed and I came upon the scene, the man had been dead for less than half an hour, proving Dorchester a liar.

Dorchester didn't want anyone else in his exclusive birder club, so he used another kind of club on the man's head to keep it that way.

HER SON AND ARSON

Detective Gibson set the cup of coffee down on the interview table for Donald Hawes, who sipped it immediately and often.

"I'm not exactly sure why I'm here," Hawes said. "I have a lot of things to attend to, you know. My mother's funeral, for one, and—" He broke down, the tears coming again, followed by the sobbing. Gibson rolled his eyes and moved the box of tissues closer.

"That's pretty much why you are here," Burton said. "We wanted to make sure you didn't have anything to tell us before your mother is buried."

"Like what?" Hawes said, honking into a tissue. "That I'm a terrible son for getting out of a burning house while my mother got left inside? OK, I'll say it."

"You just did," Gibson said. "We don't need a rerun."

"You said that the fire started in the hallway outside her room," Burton said. "So you couldn't get in to help her out."

"That's right," Hawes said miserably. "There was nothing I could do."

"Your mother was bedridden, is that right?" Gibson asked.

"Yes," Hawes said. "She was very ill. It may have been a mercy for her to pass on, you know."

"Oh, I know," Gibson muttered. "So while she was laid up in bed for the past few months, you were nice enough to cash her Social Security and pension cheques. We have the slips from the bank and the cheques, signed by you. The last one is dated 10 December, one week ago."

"We went through the proper channels for that," Hawes said, his voice still heavy with grief. "I had to pay for her medication somehow."

"What was she taking?" Burton asked. "It may be conclusive during the autopsy."

"What autopsy?" Hawes said, his voice climbing. "I didn't approve that!"

"We're grown-ups, we don't need your permission," Gibson snarled. "What was she taking?"

"Um, cyclosporine," Hawes said. "For her arthritis."

"All right, Mr Hawes," Burton said. "Please stay here with Detective Gibson. I need to check a few things in the lab, then we'll talk some more."

Burton left the two men in the interview room and headed for the lab, where Mike Trellis was waiting for him. He had just returned from the Hawes house and was covered from head to toe with ashes and soot.

"What do you see?" Trellis asked and handed

Burton a photo of Mrs Hawes's bedroom. "This was taken from the hall doorway."

"I see a guy who needs a shower and a washing machine," Burton said. "And maybe a few hours at the gym."

"Not me, the photo," Trellis said and touched his midsection. "The gym, really?"

"I see a charred body, lying supine on a burned bed, on the other side of the room," Burton said. "I see a V-shaped burn going from the bed, up the wall and onto the ceiling."

"Exactly," Trellis said. "See how the arms and legs are straight?"

"Indeed I do," said Burton. "What about the prescription?"

"Cyclosporine," Trellis said, referring to his notes. "One pill a day, same time every day. She had a 30-pill prescription, and it was last filled on 13 October."

"So if he cashed her last cheque in December," Burton said, "but hasn't filled her prescription in almost two months..."

"Someone hasn't been taking her pills," Trellis said. "Or – maybe she hasn't needed them."

"Nice work, Mike," Burton said. "Now about that shower..."

"I thought I'd do some sit-ups in your office first," Trellis said, flakes of ash falling off him with every move. "You know, because of my weight problem and everything."

"I take it back," Burton said over his shoulder as he headed back to the interview room.

"Detective Gibson won't get me any more tissues," Hawes said when Burton opened the door.

"Can't you just use imaginary ones?" Burton asked. "You know, fake tissues for fake tears?"

"What are you implying?" Hawes asked in a how-dare-you tone.

"I'm not implying anything," Burton said. "I'm telling and I'm proving. Your mother has been dead for over a month, and the fire started in her bed."

How did Burton know?

Burton's File

When a body burns, the heat from the fire dehydrates the body's muscles and causes them to contract into what is known as the "boxer's posture." Legs and arms bend, and the fists tuck beneath the chin. Mrs Hawes was lying flat on her bed, which meant that her body was already completely dehydrated before the fire started, since only death can cause that much dehydration.

Fire tends to rise and spread from its point of origin. If the flames had entered the room from the hall, they would have converged on Mrs Hawes and her bed, which were on the other side of the room. The V-shaped burn on her bedroom wall points down to her bed, indicating that's where the flame started, not where it finished.

Donald was cashing her cheques but not filling her prescriptions, and he decided to get rid of the evidence by faking her death in a fire.

IF THE CLUE FITS

Burton surveyed the living-room floor again, tilting his head this way and that to try to get a better angle. The footprints on the orange carpet told the story of what happened, but so far the tale was confusing.

"Tilt it down a little," Burton said to Trellis, who aimed the work light slightly lower. Burton studied the carpet once more, then stood up. The prints showed that someone wearing size 9 tennis shoes had walked from place to place around the room, followed by someone wearing size 12 work boots. The prints went throughout the house, but this carpet had retained the best samples.

"Let's get photos of all these prints," Burton told Trellis. "I want a left and right comparison of the smaller shoe prints, and the same for the bigger boot prints. Make sure you take the photos from directly above the print; I don't want any distortions."

"You know what's distorted?" Trellis asked. "This carpet. Who chooses an orange carpet? Someone who drops a lot of pumpkins and doesn't want the stains to show?"

"Thank you, Mike," Burton said and walked outside. Radley was taking a statement from the victim, Barry Anderson, who looked at Burton as he approached.

"Do you think you'll catch him?" Anderson asked. "He took all the jewellery, the DVD player, my work laptop, the—"

"I've got it all in the report, Mr Anderson," Radley said. "We'll do to everything we can to locate the burglar and your belongings."

"Burglar?" Anderson cried. "What about kidnapper? He grabbed me in the driveway and made me take him inside! Then he followed me around the house while I loaded all my things into my best suitcase for him! He finally left when I couldn't fit anything else in it. It got so heavy, I could barely carry it around. Can I press charges for assault, too? My shoulder's killing me!" Anderson displayed his pain by rotating his right arm at the shoulder, rubbing the area with his left hand.

"Would you like medical attention?" Radley asked.

"I think that might be for the best," Anderson said, suddenly looking very weak.

"Why don't you sit down, put your feet up?" Burton suggested. "I need to get a sample of your shoeprint, anyway, for comparison."

"Sure, whatever you need," Anderson said, and sat down on the front steps. He took off his tennis shoes, which Burton saw were size 9. He took them inside,

41

where Trellis was transferring the footprint images to his laptop.

"We can develop these photos when we get back to the lab," Trellis said. "But if you want a quick look at the best samples, I flagged them."

"Show me," Burton said. Trellis carefully made his way towards the middle of the room, careful not to disturb the path of evidence.

"See here?" he asked Burton. "The shoe prints are equally deep, but the boot prints show the right print is deeper than the left. That pattern is consistent throughout the house but, like I said, this is the best example of it."

From Trellis's tone of voice, Burton knew there was more. "What else do you have?" he said.

"How nice of you to ask," Trellis said. "Walk this way." He stepped up onto the sofa and walked across it to the other end, then peered over the back. Burton followed.

"Here we have the elusive bootus printus," Trellis whispered in a horrible Australian accent. "What a beauty she is! Notice how the print is clear from the heel to the ball of the foot, but in the toe area it gets lighter? Like the toes weren't pressed into the carpet?"

"I see it," Burton said. "Is that consistent for the rest of the prints, too?"

"Righto, mate," Trellis said, the accent still there.

"That's the worst impression I've ever heard," Burton said. "Maybe you ought to look into mime school."

Outside, Radley was watching while a pair of

EMTs looked Anderson over, squeezing his shoulder and apologizing when he yelped in pain.

"What do you think?" Radley asked as Burton returned.

"I think we need to put some handcuffs on Anderson, whether his shoulder hurts or not," Burton said.

How did Burton know?

Anderson, who was wearing the size 9 shoes, said he was forced to carry his suitcase around the house and fill it with items while the thief followed him. He also claimed this task injured his right shoulder. However, the footprints in the carpet indicated that the person wearing the *boots* did the heavy lifting with his right hand, since the right boot prints were deeper than the left.

Trellis also pointed out that the boot prints were well formed from the heel to the ball of the foot, but the toe left a very light impression. This indicates that someone was wearing boots that were too big for his feet, with the toe area of the boot having nothing in it. Anderson walked around his house in his shoes, then changed to bigger boots and retraced his steps, loading up on "stolen" items. We'll see how well he can fill the shoes of someone who tried to commit insurance fraud.

SPARKING A CONTROVERSY

"Is that the security camera's tape from the robbery?" Burton asked Mike Trellis. Trellis was sitting in front of a television in the crime lab, leaning dangerously close to the screen. Burton stood next to him and watched the crime replay in black and white.

"OK," Trellis said. "Here he is coming into the convenience store with a mask on. He pulls a revolver out of his belt and points it at the guy behind the counter and says 'Gimme all the money.' Now he's stuffing the money in his left-side jacket pocket with his free hand. Now he tells the assistant to get down and not to call the cops. The assistant gets down. He eventually does call the cops, though."

"Thanks for ruining the ending," Burton said.

"My pleasure," said Trellis, who went back to narrating the video. "The robber leaves, and we switch to camera two, which is outside the front door and shows the car park. The robber runs into the car park, sees this guy here walking towards him and he fires. We don't know if he was aiming at the guy or not, but the bullet hits the pavement about ten feet away from the walker."

Trellis froze the tape and rewound it, then played it back in slow motion. Burton could see the gun fire, and he saw the sparks that flew off the pavement where the bullet struck. "Did you recover the bullet?"

"No," Trellis said. "The sparks there are a ricochet. Even if we did find the slug, we wouldn't be able to match it to anything. Too mangled."

"What happens next?" Burton asked. Trellis continued the playback.

"After he fires the shot, the robber runs off to the right and around the corner of the store, where he's between cameras for two and a half seconds. Now, while he's invisible, you can see the guy he shot at flinch again, like he's still being shot at. But the gun only has one empty shell, and the robber didn't have time to reload, so it could be that the guy was confused and only heard one shot but thought he heard two. Then we pick up the robber with camera three, which is around the corner and shows the alley between the convenience store and the building next to it. Here, we see him run down the alley and dump the gun in the rubbish bin, where I recovered it. I can show you the footage of me, if you like. It's an award-winning performance."

"Which award?" Burton said. "Most Likely to Smell Like Rubbish for the Rest of the Day?" Trellis sniffed his shirt and frowned. "Where's the gun?" asked Burton.

"I put it on the worktable, over there," Trellis said and pointed. "The serial number has been ground away. I was hoping you could work your magnetic magic on it."

Burton found the revolver in a plastic evidence bag. The metal had fingerprint dust on it, and he could see several prints and partial prints raised by the dust.

"Did you get a match on any of these prints?" he asked.

"Not yet," said Trellis. "I'm running them through the software right now, but, like you say, 'Evidence needs more than one shoe to stand up in court. Unless it's a really big shoe that both feet can fit in.'"

"I don't think I say that," Burton said as he took the revolver out of the plastic bag. "Do you want to watch and learn over here?" Trellis stopped the tape and walked over, rubbing his eyes. "OK," Burton said, doing some narration of his own while he worked. "When the serial number gets stamped into the gun, it changes the magnetic properties of the metal around the serial number. Even if someone grinds the serial number off, the metal is still distorted from the stamping process. If we magnetize the gun, the magnetic forces will act differently around the altered metal. Then we dust the serial number area with metal powder, which collects in the altered metal and reveals the serial number."

Burton stepped back and let Trellis have a look. He saw the serial number there, written in magnetized metal shavings. "Amazing," Trellis said. "See, this is the kind of stuff that attracted me to this line of work." He looked at Burton, who just looked back.

"Get it?" Trellis asked. "Because it's a magnet, it attracted me to this job."

"Where are the bullets for this gun?" Burton asked. Trellis stepped back.

"OK, I admit it," he said. "That was a pretty bad joke, but you don't have to shoot me."

"If I was going to shoot you over a bad joke," Burton said, "you'd look like Swiss cheese by now. I just want to see if we can trace the bullet manufacturer."

Trellis handed him two evidence bags, one with five bullets and the other with one empty shell. As soon as Burton had the bullets, the technician hustled back to his television and spun the large TV so it was between him and Burton. He peeked over the top once, then disappeared.

Burton shook his head while he took the five bullets out of the bag. He picked one up and examined the back end, looking for manufacturer information, then spun the bullet and looked at the nose. The lead slug was dull under the bright laboratory lights. Burton looked at each bullet and saw that none of them had copper jackets on the tip; they were all lead slugs.

"Mike," he said. "We just ran the fingerprints and serial number from the wrong gun. The robber's trying to shoot us in the wrong direction."

How did Burton know?

Burton's File

In the security video from camera two, sparks flew off the pavement when the robber fired his pistol at the approaching man. The gun in the lab had lead slugs with no copper jackets. Lead by itself is too soft to create the tiny fragments that become sparks. Then the robber goes off camera, and the man in the car park flinches again, indicating another gunshot. That was the robber firing the second gun, with someone else's fingerprints on it. That was the gun he dumped in the bin for us to find.

STRIKE THREE, YOU'RE GUILTY!

"Vandalism?" Burton said when he and Trellis entered the small accounting office. "I think 'small nuclear explosion' is a better description." The office was in ruins, with papers, glass, desks, chairs, filing cabinets and other supplies strewn all over the floor. Just about every piece of furniture had been broken in at least one place.

"Today's Monday," Detective Radley said from the middle of the room. "Whoever broke in could have had all weekend to wreak havoc in here."

"Any suspects?" Burton asked, slipping on a pair of latex gloves from waistcoat pocket 5.

"Yes, this is interesting," Radley said. "We have two security guards in custody, and each one of them says that the other did it. They both had access to this office, and they're both clients of the accountant. The bad part is that they were both wearing leather gloves when we detained them, so chances are slim that we'll find any fingerprints here. If you ask me, we're dealing with the topic of one of the biggest chapters in my book so far: money."

Burton nodded. "When you ask why someone committed a crime, that's a pretty popular answer."

"Money is a popular answer no matter what the question is," Trellis said. "Question: Why are you still in that lousy job? Answer: The money. Question: Why don't you move to a better house? Answer: Not enough money."

"I may have found something here," Radley said from across the room. "Looks like the vandal used it as a blunt object to break the furniture."

Burton and Trellis picked their way through the office and joined Radley. "A wooden bat," Burton said. He pulled a fingerprint brush out of waistcoat pocket 16 and print powder out of 22. "Mike, take some photos and video of the bat while I get ready to dust it for prints."

"Sure thing," Trellis said and got to work. Burton and Radley waited, looking at him. He stopped taking photos and looked back at them.

"What?" he said. "Do I have something on my face?"

"We're waiting," said Radley.

"Waiting for what?" Trellis said, confused.

"We know you've got one," Burton said. "Just get on with it so we can continue."

"I don't know what you're talking—" Trellis started, then stopped. "Oh, wait. You mean one of my hilarious jokes that lighten the mood and make everyone happy?"

"That's not how I would describe them," Burton said. "But we're still waiting."

"I'm hurt, you guys," Trellis said, resuming his photography. "This is a serious crime, and you expect me to joke about it." Burton and Radley looked at each other, both of them a bit embarrassed.

Trellis shook his head. "Some perpetrator could be on the loose right now, committing foul play as we speak. Get it? Foul play? Because he used a bat."

Burton and Radley groaned but were relieved to have the most painful part of the investigation out of the way. When Trellis was done with the photography, Burton moved in with the print kit. He dusted the length of the bat, but no obvious prints showed up.

"Nothing?" Radley said over his shoulder.

"I wouldn't say that." Burton pointed to a pattern in the powder. "What does that look like to you?"

Radley tilted her head to one side, then the other. "It looks like a contact print, like the bat was pressed against someone's skin. But we can't match that to anything. It could be from anywhere, on anyone's body!"

"I'm not taking prints off a security guard's entire body," Trellis said.

"That won't be necessary," Burton said. "I don't need to see the guards. I only need their gloves."

How will Burton match the print to the vandal?

Even though the vandal was wearing gloves, he still left a distinctive print. Leather is animal hide, and it leaves a print just like any other skin. By matching the leather glove to the print on the bat, the vandal was easy to identify. To quote Trellis at the time of the arrest: "The guy didn't just like his bat. He gloved it."

THE CORPORATE CORPSE

The cubicles were about the same size as Burton's CSI truck, and the technical writers were packed in four to a cube. They clacked away on their keyboards, most of them wearing headphones and sipping cups of water from the cooler at the end of the office aisle. Burton peered over the top of the cubicle walls and saw that they covered the entire office floor.

"How many people work in this office?" he asked Ellen North, who was his escort. The pharmaceutical company didn't allow outsiders to wander around the plant alone, for security and confidentiality reasons.

"There are approximately 300 employees on this floor," North said. "But in the entire building? I'd have to check."

"Does everyone in the building have access to this area?" Detective Radley asked.

"No," North said. "If they don't work on this floor or have special access, they can't get into this room."

Burton nodded, knowing that policy is one thing but reality is another. "Do you know if Mr Bell had any arguments or conflicts with an employee recently?" Bell was currently being photographed by Mike Trellis in the toilets where his body had been discovered two hours ago. From the state of the toilets, Bell had obviously been nauseous along with some bowel issues, and the sudden onset of the symptoms waved a big flag at the crew that said poison. Trellis had guessed arsenic, and Burton thought he could be right.

"No one reported anything," North said. "But it's a time of high stress. We do have a big deadline approaching, and if we don't complete our work on time, production will have to stop until we do. This morning the photocopier broke down, which didn't help the situation. But Mr Bell remained calm and kept to business as usual, right down to his three cups of coffee with lots of creamer. He even dipped his tie in his coffee cup like always. He was kind of clumsy that way."

Radley thought their escort might tear up at the memory, but North just shrugged and continued.

"All of his employees were on track with their annual goals and performance reviews, so there shouldn't have been any problems," she finished, as if that were the end of the topic.

"Thank you, Miss North," Radley said. "We'll let you know if we need anything."

"Oh, I'm afraid I can't leave you unescorted," North said. "Corporate policy."

"Understood," Radley said with a tight smile. She

looked at Burton, who had a grin of his own. They started walking towards the toilets.

"This reminds me of the Halloway case," Burton said, pulling a name out of the air. "Do you remember that one?"

"How could I forget?" Radley said, ducking her head to stifle a chuckle. North was one step behind them, well within earshot.

"The way his head kept oozing that stuff," Burton said and looked around at North. "It's amazing what happens when a mucous membrane is stimulated with electricity. That was a lot of snot, let me tell you. Almost five gallons." North nodded, swallowed, and slowed her pace enough to let Burton and Radley get about ten feet in front of her.

"Snot?" Radley asked under her breath.

"It's the first thing I thought of," Burton murmured as they turned the corner to the toilets. On the right was the open doorway to the copy room, and Burton saw a technician working on the bulky machine. He and Radley made a detour into the copy room, North right behind them.

"Hello, I'm Wes Burton with the crime lab and this is Detective Radley."

"I didn't do it," the repairman said.

"You didn't do what?" Burton asked.

"Whatever happened."

"Do you know what happened this morning?" asked Radley.

"Look, guys," the repairman said, turning around. "I'm working on this as fast as I can, and I got people coming in here every five minutes to see if it's ready yet. I even skipped my morning break to keep working, so no, I don't know what happened, but I do know I didn't do it, because I've been in here all day. And once I do get it working, I still have this mess to clean up." He gestured at the table next to the copier, where several toner cartridges sat surrounded by powder that had leaked from them. At the back of the table were a coffee machine and various creamers and sugar replacements, along with a stack of foam cups and thin red stirrers.

"How long have these cartridges been here?" Burton asked.

"I pulled them out first thing," the repairman said, his head back in the machine.

"Can I have some coffee?" Burton asked North, who nodded. He leaned over the table and plucked a cup off the stack, then leaned farther to grab the pot and pour the hot coffee. To reach the creamer, he practically had to bend at a 90-degree angle.

"You're under arrest for murder," Burton told the cup of coffee and took a sip.

How did Bell get poisoned?

Bell had three cups of coffee that morning, with creamer. When I got a cup for myself, I had to bend over the table to reach everything. The table was covered in toner powder, which contains antimony, an element that causes symptoms similar to arsenic poisoning. Bell leaned over the table and dragged his tie through the powder, then accidentally dipped his tie in his coffee. Bell poisoned himself and didn't even realize it.

CRIME FILE INVESTIGATIONS

THE CRIME IS A MATTER OF TIME

"This is an odd one," Burton said and held up a file. Mike Trellis and Dr Crown were in the crime lab examining a body. They both looked up.

"More odd than this guy?" Trellis asked. "He jumped out of a moving car at 60 miles an hour, fell into a ditch and somehow managed to catch himself on fire. Twice."

"Maybe not as odd as that," Burton said. "But this is still a bit different than normal. Paula Larson, 42, just confessed to the 18 January murder of her fiancé, Denny Washington. She gave us the how and the why – she shot him with his own shotgun because he was stealing from her and was going to break up with her just before the wedding."

"So why are we involved?" said Trellis. "Sounds like everything is taken care of."

"Not quite," Burton said. "She claims it was a crime of passion, that she didn't plan to kill him. We have to prove her right or wrong. If it was premeditated, that makes it first-degree murder. If not, she might only get charged with voluntary manslaughter."

Trellis looked at Dr Crown. "Do you take offence to that? The fact that it's always 'manslaughter,' whether the people involved were male or female?"

"No," Crown said.

"Do you take offence to anything?" asked Trellis. Crown extracted the heart from the corpse and held it for a moment, pondering the question.

"I don't appreciate being referred to as a coroner," she said. "I'm a forensic pathologist." Burton and Trellis both saw that she was unconsciously squeezing the heart while she thought about being called a coroner.

Trellis looked at Burton nervously. "Let's leave the forensic pathologist to her work, shall we?"

"Good idea," Burton said. The two of them went to the other side of the lab, where they surveyed the evidence in the Paula Larson case.

"Larson panicked after she shot Washington," Burton said, pointing to a set of bloodstained bedsheets in sealed plastic bags. "Her statement says she pulled the bottom sheet off her bed, wrapped his body in it and put the whole bundle into the boot of her car. She drove around looking for a place to hide the body, but guilt overcame her and she drove to the police department instead."

"I wish all killers would be that courteous," Trellis said. "Tell her, next time she should bring a pizza, too."

"I'll pass it along," Burton said. "We also have the shotgun, the shell recovered from the scene and the clothes both of them wore at the time of the shooting."

"I'll take a look at the clothes," Trellis said. "Just to make sure the gunshot residue and blood spatter match up with what she says happened."

"Don't assume anything she says is true," Burton said. "We need to learn for ourselves which shoes fit this evidence. I'll examine the sheet; you let me know if you find anything."

They got to work, with Trellis laying out the clothes and checking bloodstain patterns. Burton did the same with the sheet, peering closely at the side of the fabric that had come in contact with Washington's body.

"I've got some fibres here," Burton said, plucking the fuzzy brown strands off the sheet with a pair of tweezers. "They look like paper, but I'll have to check them out under the microscope. Have you found anything yet?"

"Nothing to help or hurt Larson's case," Trellis said. "I did find a grocery receipt in her trouser pocket dated 17 January, the day before the shooting. But it only has stuff on it like eggs, milk, bread, cereal and so on. If she had purchased a copy of *How to Kill Your Fiancé and Get Away with It*, we might have something."

Burton was too busy looking into the microscope to respond. "These fibres are brown paper," he said. "Is there anything on Washington's clothes that could have transferred these fibres to the sheet?"

"No," Trellis said. "I found some lint and fuzz, but no brown-paper fibres."

"Hold on a minute," Burton said, and went back to the sheet. He examined the photos he had taken before touching anything in the boot and spread the sheet out in the exact same way. Then he stood where Larson would have been when she put Washington's body into the car. "Washington was wrapped in the sheet like a burrito," he said, and mimicked lifting the body onto the sheet, then covering it as Larson had. "She pulled the top part of the sheet over him first, then covered that with the bottom part. So only the top flap actually contacted Washington's body. I recovered the fibres from the bottom flap, so they couldn't have come from him. They were already on the sheet when his body entered the boot." Burton looked intently at Trellis. "I want you to go down to the interview room and ask Larson one question."

"Did you plan to kill your fiancé?" Trellis tried.

"No," Burton said. "Paper or plastic?"

How will the answer affect Larson's case?

Burton's File

The brown-paper fibres found on the sheet are from a grocery bag. Their presence on the fabric indicates that the sheet was in Larson's boot on January 17, a day before the murder. Larson put the sheet there knowing she was going to kill Washington eventually, but in the meantime, she continued to place the usual things, such as groceries, in her boot. Trellis referred to the whole situation as a "Gross series of events. Get it? Gross series ... groceries."

THE EVIDENCE WILL FLOAT

Gibson poked at a stack of boxes on the workbench, and they almost toppled over.

"What's in these?" he asked.

"I haven't checked yet," Burton answered. "And if you knock them over, they'll be tainted evidence and inadmissible in court." The two of them were in Ron Carney's garage workshop, but Carney wasn't with them. He was in the interview room at the police station with Radley, waiting for his lawyer to show up before he said anything.

"So do you think this guy is our thief?" Gibson said, clearly bored with the process of gathering evidence. Burton sighed, knowing that Gibson would continue to ask questions and make worthless remarks to pass the time.

"He fits the profile we're looking for," he responded, happy at least to be talking about the case rather than cars, Gibson's favorite topic.

"He lives alone, has experience with tools and working with his hands, and has a few expensive items in his house that don't seem affordable for someone on his salary."

"Ever hear of credit cards?" Gibson asked.

"He doesn't have any," Burton said. "Which shows another trait we're looking for: a mistrust of the financial system."

"So how does he get into the places he robs?" Gibson said, flicking a light switch on and off.

"Don't do that, please," Burton said. "One of the reasons we're here is to see if we can find out how he gains access to the buildings without breaking in. Keep your eye open for keys, access cards, fake uniforms..."

"What if he crawled in through the air ducts?" said Gibson.

"Air ducts are designed to hold air, not men," Burton said. "He'd crash through the ceiling before he crawled ten feet. I'd like to think we didn't overlook something like that." Burton photographed a large piece of cardboard with bricks at the four corners, then moved all of that aside. Beneath was a four-foot-square table, the top covered with a flat piece of tin. He took a picture of that as well, then moved on.

"I see a small vacuum cleaner over here," Gibson said. "Should I at least clean up while I'm here? I feel kind of useless just standing around."

"You're not satisfied with your role of blocking my light and introducing offending odours into the crime scene?" Burton asked.

"I finished that job in the first 15 minutes," Gibson retorted. "Do you want to see what's in the vacuum cleaner or not?"

"I'm giddy with excitement," Burton said and took a photo of the small cleaner. "OK, open it up. Slowly, please." Gibson did so, and Burton saw the glitter of glass pieces in the cleaner's filter and tank. He took a few evidence bags out of waistcoat pocket 9 and slipped a sample of the glass into each one.

"I think I might know how he's getting in and out without leaving a trace," Burton said. "At least, not one we can see with the naked eye. Let's go to the last robbery location and see if I'm right."

At Main Street Party Supplies, the most recent business on the serial thief's hit list, Burton and Gibson stood outside the shop front and looked at the windows. It was 10 o'clock at night and the shop was dark.

"See anything special?" Burton asked.

"Only you," Gibson said, then shook his head. "I don't see anything here. I don't even know what I'm looking for."

Burton reached into waistcoat pocket 25 and pulled out his handheld ultraviolet light. He snapped it on and waved it along the windows until he reached the one closest to the door. The glass fluoresced under the black light, glowing a soft green. Burton turned off the light and measured the window.

"Four feet by four feet," he said. "Let's get back to the station. Whatever alibi Carney has, it's going to be as transparent as this piece of glass."

How did Burton know?

Carney scouted his targets and measured their windows before breaking in. He took those measurements home and made a window exactly the same size as the one he intended to break, using a technique that involved pouring hot molten glass over liquid tin. When the "float glass" cools, it has small amounts of the tin on one side, which causes it to fluoresce, or glow, under black light. The four-foot-square tin table in Carney's workshop matched the four-foot-square window at Main Street Party Supplies.

THE FROZEN FISHERMAN

Burton sat across from the suspect, Wally Potts, who was currently blowing his nose into a tissue. Gibson slouched in the corner behind Potts, his arms folded. He called this arrangement "The Hammer and the Anvil," because Burton laid the base of evidence out for the suspect, and Gibson smashed them against it with good old interrogation.

"Mr Potts," Burton said. "This is what we know, just so we don't waste each other's time. You and Grant were the only ones in the ice-fishing shack. The bruising on Grant's neck indicates he was suffocated from behind in a choke hold. Grant was found in the shack two days later by a park ranger, his body frozen stiff." Burton hoped this wealth of information would stun Potts into a confession.

"Stiff, that's funny," Potts said, sniffing. "Is that where the term comes from? Stiff, because the body is frozen?"

"No, it comes from rigor mortis," Burton said, "the chemical process that takes place in the muscles after death. The chemicals contract the muscles to make them rigid, locking the body in position. There are plenty of factors, but generally speaking, if the temperature is around 21 degrees, the body will go from limp to completely stiff and back to limp again within 48 hours. But Grant's body hasn't gone through that process yet, because it was frozen soon after death. Now tell us what happened."

"Yeah," Gibson said. "Before he gets out his slide projector and starts lecturing about trace fibres and blood spatters."

"That isn't until after lunch," Burton said. "Mr Potts? We're waiting."

"Here's the deal," Potts said. "Grant and I went ice fishing on Sunday at his shack on the lake. I left before Grant did, and the last I saw of him, he was still sitting with his line in the water. That's all I know, and I'm not saying anything else." Potts coughed, covering his mouth with the crook of his elbow.

"Don't get me sick," Gibson said. "You think I'm grumpy now, you ought to see me with the flu."

Burton shuddered at the thought. "How long have you had this cold?" he asked Potts. Potts considered the question for a moment to see if it was a trick.

"I came down with it on Friday," he said after deciding his sniffles couldn't incriminate him. Again, he coughed into the bend of his elbow.

"The contagious phase is two to four days," Burton told Gibson. "It's Wednesday, so we should be in the clear."

"Does that mean I can get in his face?" Gibson asked, a grin spreading across his own.

"You can do whatever you want," Burton said. "I'm going to take Mr Potts's shirt to the lab and prove he killed Grant."

How will Burton do it?

Mr Potts had been ill since Friday, which means he was coughing in the ice shack on Sunday. He showed a habit of using the crook of his elbow to stifle his coughs, leaving plenty of DNA on his sleeve. Grant was suffocated from behind using a choke hold, which places the crook of the elbow's attacker against the victim's throat. A swab of Grant's neck, which had been frozen and preserved since the murder, showed a match to Potts's DNA, proving that Potts killed Grant. Gibson did end up with a cold, but it was due to his tendency to not wash his hands as often as he should.

THE GUILTY FIRST
IMPRESSION

"We need some impressions of those shoe prints in the mud outside," Burton said. He was standing in a huge barn next to the body of Kendall Luthey, who had been killed within the last 24 hours.

"OK," Mike Trellis said. He found a clean spot on the floor and lay down. Detective Gibson walked in, looked at Trellis, and stopped.

"What are you doing?" he asked.

"This is my impression of a shoe print," Trellis said. "Get it? Because I'm on the ground."

Gibson looked at Burton. "Can I shoot him?" he asked, pointing at Trellis.

"I'd rather you didn't," Burton said. "He still owes me for lunch yesterday. And he's going to have to skip lunch today if he doesn't get moving." Trellis scampered off to get the impression kit from the van.

"Any leads yet on who may have been here with Luthey?" Burton asked as he snapped photos of the body. He noticed that Luthey's hands were very clean, with manicured nails. If there was any trace evidence under those nicely trimmed nails, it would be easy to spot.

"We ran the phone records," Gibson said. "One number was on there six times in the last day, and it belongs to a Mr Evan Akers, who I just spoke with. He's on his way over right now. He says he was here last night, but when he left, Luthey was alive and well. Apparently, they were working on some new engine design that they're going to patent." Gibson pointed towards a worktable covered with a tarpaulin. "That's probably the engine. Want to have a look?"

"Not unless it becomes part of the investigation," Burton said. "Why is Akers coming here? He can't access the scene until we're done."

"He probably wants to make sure we don't steal his precious engine design. To be honest, I don't see how they could make one better than the Chevy Big Block V8," Gibson said.

"I don't even know what that means," Burton said, and headed out to see how Trellis was doing.

The mud had retained the shoe prints well, and Trellis had set up an angled light next to the prints to bring out their depth and detail. He was finishing up with the photography when Burton and Gibson joined him.

"These are good plastic prints," Burton said.

"Plastic?" said Gibson. "How can you tell the shoes were plastic? Like clown shoes?" Trellis almost dropped the impression kit he was carrying. He despised clowns.

"No," Burton said. "There are three basic types of shoe prints: patent, latent and plastic. Patent means they're visible, like when someone walks through wet paint. Latent means they're invisible to the naked eye. Those happen, for example, when someone walks across a concrete floor and leaves traces from the soles of their shoes. Plastic prints, like these here, occur when you walk through soft materials like mud, snow or sand and leave a three-dimensional print behind."

Trellis set a wooden frame around one of the shoe prints and was about to pour dental stone plaster in when Burton interrupted.

"You might want to spray it first, Mike," he said. Trellis nodded in agreement, then sprayed the shoeprint with clear shellac to harden the mud. Burton looked at Gibson, who seemed confused. "It helps keep the print from being distorted by the weight of the plaster," he told the detective.

"I know," Gibson said, quite unconvincingly.

"Right," said Burton. "Then you probably noticed that these particular prints have a distinct angle to them. The toe end of the shoe is much deeper than the heel."

"Of course," Gibson said. A large pickup truck pulled up in front of the barn. A skinny man with a greasy baseball hat jumped down from the driver's seat and strode towards them.

"That's close enough, Mr Akers," Gibson said. "This is still a crime scene."

"Did you look under that tarp?" Akers demanded, pointing an oil-stained finger at them.

"What tarp?" Gibson answered. Burton was slightly amused – Gibson's approach to conversation was fun to listen to, unless he was talking to you.

"That engine is worth a lot of money," Akers said. "If you try to steal my idea, there's going to be trouble."

"Did Luthey try to steal your idea?" asked Gibson. Akers started to talk then caught himself.

"We were business partners," he said. "Fifty-fifty, that was the deal."

"Now, let's see," Gibson said. "I was never good at maths, more of a woodwork guy. But 50 per cent plus 50 per cent … that means you now get 100 per cent, right?"

"When I left here last night," Akers said, pointing that oily finger at the ground, "he was alive."

"Are these your shoe prints, Mr Akers?" Burton asked, indicating the series of indentations that led from the barn. Akers had left a fresh set of tracks from his truck when he approached them, and Burton could tell they were the same, though not nearly as deep in the toe end as the older prints.

Akers looked at the prints, then his shoes. "I guess they are," he said.

"And when you left last night, Luthey was fine? You weren't in any hurry to leave?" asked Burton.

"That's right."

"Then why were you running away from the barn?"

How did Burton know?

Last night's shoe prints were deeper in the toe than they were in the heel, indicating that Akers had most of his weight on the front of his feet, as humans do when they run. The tracks he left from the truck when he showed up at the crime scene were flat, and demonstrated what type of prints he left when he walked.

Akers's oily hands indicated that he did most of the work, while Luthey's clean hands and manicured fingernails suggested that he did not help much when it came to the labour. Akers felt that if they didn't split the work 50-50, they shouldn't split the money 50-50. In the argument that followed, Akers killed Luthey.

THE LIFE-SAVING STOMACH

"Stop pacing, you're making me nervous," Detective Radley said.

"Sorry," Burton grumbled. "I don't like hospitals. They smell like sickness."

"So you prefer the smell of death over illness? That's pretty morbid," said Radley. "Do you know why you feel that way?"

Burton frowned at this for a moment, started to answer, then stopped. "Wait a minute," he said. "Are you asking out of concern, or are you looking for content for your book?"

"Both," Radley admitted. "I'm starting to work out that criminals might not be as interesting as those who catch them."

Before Burton could comment on this, Dr Felson emerged from the room in front of them.

"He's awake, but weak," Felson said. "If you need to speak with him, please make it short."

"Thank you, Doctor," Radley said as she opened the door. Burton followed, his hands in his pockets. He knew it was ridiculous, but he was wary of touching anything.

"Hello Mr Kuhn, I'm Detective Radley. This is Wes Burton, he's a criminalist with our CSI lab. We'd like to ask you a few questions, if you're up for it."

"Sure, sure," Kuhn said. "Did I do something wrong?"

"Well," Burton said. "You didn't die."

"Beg pardon?" Kuhn said, leaning forwards in his bed.

"We believe you were poisoned," Radley said, stepping in front of Burton and his poor bedside manner. "Someone gave you a lethal dose of cyanide, and we'd like to find out who."

"And how you survived the dosage," Burton added over her shoulder.

"OK," Kuhn said. "Where do we start?"

Radley took out her notepad. "How about a list of everything you had to eat or drink in the last few days?"

"Wow, let's see," Kuhn started. "Today's Thursday, so on Monday, I had, let's see ... grits and toast for breakfast, with OJ..." Kuhn continued with his list, compiling items that Burton would expect to see on a billy goat's menu. "Tuesday night I had tuna and broccoli, with pink lemonade to drink. Then on Wednesday, I had ... wait, I didn't eat anything yesterday. Except those biscuits. I can't resist a good biscuit. Especially when they have almonds in them."

"Why didn't you eat anything else?" Radley asked.

"I ran out of my medication," Kuhn said. "I have to take betaine hydrochloride as a supplement. I have a stomach-acid deficiency, and without my medicine, I can't really digest anything."

Burton looked at the chart at the foot of Kuhn's bed. "Hypochlorhydria," he read. "Your stomach doesn't produce enough hydrochloric acid."

"Yeah, that's right." Kuhn said. "How long do you think I'll have to stay here? I'm afraid if I'm gone too long, my landlady will throw my stuff in the street and let my apartment to someone else."

"Did you and your landlady have an argument?" Radley asked, her pen poised above the notepad.

"Nah," Kuhn said, waving his hand. "It's in the lease that she can't raise my rent, so she's always teasing me about moving out so she can get a new tenant at a higher rate. But she doesn't really want me to leave. Heck, she baked me those biscuits, so she must like me a little."

"You still might have to sign a new lease, though," Burton said. "After all, she won't be a very good landlady from prison."

How did Burton know she gave Kuhn the poison, and how did he survive?

Kuhn mentioned that he couldn't resist the almond biscuits the landlady made for him. Cyanide has a distinctive bitter almond odour that the would-be killer covered up by adding almonds to the poisoned biscuits. What the landlady didn't know was that Kuhn was off his medication and his stomach was not producing any hydrochloric acid, which is needed to start the chemical reaction that makes cyanide fatal.

THE MISSING MERRILL

Burton met Dr Crown in the lab's examination room and was surprised to find her in a very good mood.

"What are you so happy about?" he asked her.

"What makes you think I'm overly happy?" Crown asked back.

"You put an exclamation mark on the note you left me," Burton said. "You wrote 'Meet me in the lab right away!' For you, that's like sending a parade and fleet of hot-air balloons."

Crown looked at him a moment, seemingly upset that someone knew how she felt, then a small smile appeared. "Mrs Merrill is here."

"Aha!" Burton said. "I should have known! You always get excited when we have to exhume a body."

"Well," Crown said. "We have the opportunity to possibly provide closure for those who are still grieving."

"And find a clue that someone else missed," Burton added.

"Yes, that too," Crown said. "She's right over here." Crown and Burton walked to the farthest table in the examination room, where Mike Trellis was waiting with the body.

"Your first exhumed autopsy?" Burton asked him.

"Yup," Trellis said. "I guess this is as close as I'm going to get to examining a mummy."

"Michael," Crown said. "Do you remember the talk we had about respect in the presence of the deceased?"

"Yes, Dr Crown," Trellis said.

"Good. Now let's see what those inept jokers missed the first time around," said Crown.

"I read the file on this the other day," Burton said, securing his gloves and gown. "Mrs Merrill died 13 years ago, at age 57. She didn't receive an autopsy or even a wake before her funeral, and her husband asked for a closed-casket burial. Didn't any of that strike investigators as odd? Something they might want to look into?"

"At the time," Crown said, "Mr Merrill was a powerful individual. He could have put pressure on certain people to make the whole thing go away as soon as possible." Crown opened the case file and pulled out a newspaper clipping that showed Mr and Mrs Merrill next to each other at the 1986 dedication of a new library. The tall man did strike an imposing figure, with Mrs Merrill only coming up to his chest.

"Where is old man Merrill now?" Trellis asked.

"I believe he's at the courthouse as we speak,

trying to stop us from pulling this sheet back," Crown said as she pulled the sheet back.

Something caught Burton's eye.

"Mike, do you have the X-rays that the lab took of Mrs Merrill this morning?" he asked.

"They're in the file," Trellis said. Burton flipped through and found the X-rays, sorted them until he found the films of the humerus bones, and measured them.

"How tall is Mr Merrill?" Burton asked the room.

"I've stood next to him," Crown said. "I'd put him at six-foot-two, give or take an inch."

"That's 74 inches," Burton muttered to himself. "In the photo, Mrs Merrill comes up to his chest, which looks to be about three quarters of his height. So we'll put her at..."

"Fifty-five and a half inches," Trellis said.

Burton looked at the X-ray again. "Dr Crown, will you please measure the upper arm bones on the body?"

Crown did, and reported her findings. "Right humerus is 13.25 inches, left humerus is 13 inches," she said.

"Call down to the courthouse and have Mr Merrill detained," Burton said. "We need to ask him where his wife is. This isn't Mrs Merrill."

How did he know?

A person's height is usually five times the length of their humerus (upper arm) bone. If Mrs Merrill was only 55.5 inches tall, or approximately four foot six inches, her humerus would be 11 inches long instead of 13. Desiccation occurs as the body decomposes, which means the bones dry out and shrink. Even after this happened, the body in Mrs Merrill's casket was at least a foot too tall.

THE PENCIL POINTS

Burton and Detective Gibson walked towards the small, cosy house on Cedar Street and saw a grey-haired man peek at them through the drapes, then duck back quickly.

"We've been spotted," Gibson said.

"Should we call for backup?" Burton asked.

"I don't think we need the SWAT team to handle Mr Tanner," said Gibson, glancing down at Burton. "Besides, if he attacks, he'll go for the weaker-looking one of us first."

"I'll try to save you," Burton said, leaving Gibson with a scowl on his face. He knocked on the front door. The same grey-haired man peered through the curtained window in the door, and Burton could hear the sound of several locks being undone. The door inched open, and the man pressed his face into the crack.

"Yeah?" he said.

"Are you Ralph Tanner?" Burton asked.

"What's it to ya?" the old man said. Gibson stepped next to Burton on the front steps, and the old man gave him a distrusting glare.

"I'm Detective Gibson; pleased to meet you," Gibson said. "This guy here, you can call him Burton. He's from the crime lab."

Burton said, "Mr Tanner, we just left the hospital where your wife has been admitted for emergency care. She had stomach pain and fits of vomiting and she said that she thought you might be trying to kill her."

"If I was trying, she'd be dead!" Tanner spat and slammed the door shut.

"Nice work, Burton," Gibson said. "Now he's probably inside destroying evidence and our careers."

"Your career was ruined anyway," Burton said. He eyed the two rubbish bins along the curb in front of Tanner's house. "Doesn't the area between the path and the road belong to the city?" he asked.

"Yeah, why?" Gibson said.

"Because maybe the evidence we're looking for isn't inside anymore," said Burton as he snapped on a pair of latex gloves from waistcoat pocket 5. He handed a pair to Gibson, who took them like they were radioactive.

"This isn't part of my job description," Gibson said.

"Come on," said Burton. "Maybe you'll find a shirt you like. Or something for lunch." They lifted the lids off the rubbish bins and were greeted immediately by the stench of warm filth.

"Reminds me of your aftershave," Burton said as he started sifting through the rubbish.

"Gacch, this is horrible!" Gibson said. "What are we looking for, anyway?"

"Mrs Tanner said her husband kept telling her she needed more tea," Burton said, lifting a cluster of old tea bags out of the bin. He placed them in an evidence bag from waistcoat pocket 9. "She said it was kind of sludgy and tasted like it had dirt in it, or clay. She said the more she drank, the sicker she felt. Finally, she drove herself to the hospital when Mr Tanner refused to take her. He said she just needed more tea."

"How romantic," Gibson said. "Maybe he was using all these pencils to write her love letters." Gibson was steadily making a pile of broken pencils he found in the rubbish.

"That's a lot of pencils to throw away at one time," Burton said. Even though they were in pieces, he could tell there were at least 20 pencils so far.

"Well, no wonder they were tossed," Gibson said. "They're hollow." He squinted into the end of one of the segments, then passed it to Burton. The CSI looked at the piece, and sure enough, the centre was empty.

"Get ready to kick that door in if you have to," Burton said. "These pencils just wrote Mr Tanner's arrest warrant for attempted murder."

How did Burton know?

Burton's File

Mr Tanner removed the cores of the pencils, crushed them into powder and mixed it into Mrs Tanner's tea, thinking it would give her lead poisoning. What he didn't know is that pencil lead actually contains no lead and never has; it's made from a mixture of graphite and clay. He only succeeded in giving her an upset stomach – and a husband in prison.

THE PROOF IS HEAR

Dr Crown looked up briefly when Burton entered the examination room, then went back to her microscope. She was expecting his visit but not the company he had with him.

"Dr Crown, this is Gary Reardon," Burton said by way of introduction. "He's with the insurance company that covered Benny Owens." Burton gestured towards the body on the table, which was covered with a white sheet.

"Why are you here?" Crown asked Reardon. She didn't appreciate meddling in her lab, and tours were absolutely out of the question.

"Mr Burton here says that you have proof that Mr Owens did not jump to his death on purpose. That he fell," Reardon said. "Of course, my company doesn't cover suicide, so it's relevant to the surviving family and the company."

"Burton, is this true?" Crown asked, peering at

him over her glasses. Burton seemed instantly uncomfortable. He knew it would bother Crown to have Reardon in her lab, but he was beginning to worry that she might kick them both out.

"Well, um," he started. "Mr Reardon wasn't going to take my word for it, so I offered to show him the proof. And the proof's in here. So here we are." It sounded lame to his ears, and he could only imagine what Crown thought of his logic. She looked from him to Reardon and back again, then walked to the examination table.

"Let's get this over with," she muttered, much to Burton's relief.

"OK, Mr Reardon," Burton said as they approached the body. "Owens was setting up a four-storey scaffold when he fell. That means he was working on the top of the tower as it was being built, so there were no rails or safety wires. He was wearing earplugs, eye protection and a hard hat. He also should have been tied off, but that's not relevant. Shoulda woulda coulda."

"We've been over all of this," Reardon said. "We know he was in dangerous working conditions, but so was everyone else, and they didn't fall. Owens had a history of depression, and he and his wife weren't getting along very well at the time of his death. Nothing that I've seen indicates his fall was accidental."

"Then take a look at this," Burton said, and pulled the sheet away from Owens's head. He was hoping Reardon would cringe, look away, or at least lose the smug smile he had on his face. Instead, he leaned towards the body and shook his head.

"What am I looking for?" Reardon said, his tone suggesting he was a bit bored.

"You're looking for his hearing," Burton said, and handed him an otoscope with the light on. Reardon held the cone outside of Owens's left ear, peered through the lens, and stood up.

"I see an ear," Reardon said, with a roll of his eyes. "This is groundbreaking." Crown took the otoscope from him and inserted the cone almost all the way into Owens's ear.

"Look again," she said. Reardon did, and when he stood up this time, he was frowning. Burton smiled.

"I'm not a doctor," Reardon said. "But it doesn't look good in there."

"Otitis media," Burton said. "Or inflammation of the middle ear, if you prefer. The initial postmortem examination didn't catch it because he was such a mess from the fall. But after a thorough cleaning, Dr Crown saw the infection."

Reardon considered this for a moment, then looked at Crown. "Nice work, Doctor. I'll pass the news on to the company. We'll deem Mr Owens's death accidental."

What convinced Reardon?

At the time of his death, Owens had a serious middle-ear infection and was wearing earplugs, which made the problem worse. If the outer and middle ear are healthy, they contain the same amount of atmospheric pressure (when you yawn and hear a pop, that's your middle ear equalizing the pressure). If the middle ear is infected, it cannot equalize the pressure and cannot transmit signals to the inner ear. The inner ear is very important when it comes to maintaining balance, something Owens needed to keep him from falling.

THE SHATTERED LIE

"Good fences make good neighbours," Burton said while he snapped photos of Kevin Mahoney's living room. Glass from the shattered picture window covered the carpet, and a large brick sat in the middle of the broken shards.

"These guys would need a pretty big fence," Detective Radley said. "I'm talking Berlin Wall big."

"I was thinking the Great Wall of China," Burton said. "Let's see if we have this right. Mahoney says that he was watching TV when he saw his neighbour, Cliff Adams, in his front garden. Mahoney starts yelling at him through the window to get off his property, and Adams picks up this brick and chucks it through the window, shouting that he's going to kill Mahoney. So Mahoney grabs the .22 rifle he keeps above the fireplace and shoots Adams in the leg."

"That's what Mahoney says," said Radley.

"According to Adams, he was walking through Mahoney's front garden – which he admits Mahoney doesn't like – when Mahoney starts yelling at him through the picture window. Adams ignores him and keeps walking, and Mahoney shoots at him through the window, striking him in the leg. Adams goes down, but manages to pick up this brick and throw it at Mahoney to try to keep him from firing again."

"So it's a case of he-said-he-said," Burton remarked. "Who do you believe?"

"I think they're both full of it," Radley said. "We have records of police responding to multiple calls because these two can't live next door to each other without breaking into civil war every now and then. But one of them is flat-out lying."

Burton finished with his camera and took an evidence bag out of waistcoat pocket 9. He slipped a few samples of the glass into the bag and sealed it. "Let's take a closer look at this brick," he said, taking a brush out of waistcoat pocket 16 and fingerprint powder out of pocket 22. "Before I start, do you see anything special about this brick?" he asked Radley. She leaned in for a closer look. The brick was the standard size, shape and colour, with nothing on the surface but a little dirt from the front garden. Radley shook her head.

"Looks like a plain old brick to me," she said.

Burton nodded and began to dust for prints. When he was finished, there were three good fingerprints, one that was a bit smeared and one good thumb print. "The thrower was left-handed," Burton said. "Is Adams a southpaw?"

"He is," Radley said, "And there was dirt on his left hand. We also have gunshot residue on Mahoney's right hand, so we know he's right-handed."

Burton picked up the brick and bagged it, careful to leave the bits of glass that were underneath it in place.

"So we know that Mahoney did shoot the gun," Radley continued, "and that Adams did throw the brick, but in what order? It's Adams's word against Mahoney's."

"No," Burton said. "It's Mahoney's word against the truth. He's the one who's lying."

How did Burton know?

Mahoney claimed he shot at Adams after his neighbour threw the brick through the window. However, the brick had no glass on top of it but did have pieces of glass beneath it, indicating that the window was already broken when the brick landed on the floor.

The glass in the living room also implicates Mahoney as the one who acted first. Ordinary glass is classified as a fluid and flexes like a trampoline when a bullet hits it. When the glass snapped back from the bullet's impact, the window shattered and the pieces sprayed into the living room.

THE TOILET TANK TEST

"You already know what happened, don't you?" Trellis said as soon as he saw Burton in the large bathroom. He just had that look on his face.

"I might," Burton said with a small smile. "Let's see if you can figure it out." Trellis frowned. He didn't mind Burton's surprise tests, but he knew he was on a tight schedule. Burton wouldn't let quiz time interfere with procedure.

"Can I get some more light in here?" Trellis asked. The bulb in the ceiling fixture above the toilet was missing, and the room was dimly lit by the hall light.

"If you need it," Burton said, not quite mocking but close. The frown on Trellis's face deepened, and he stepped into the bathroom.

"That is an extraordinary amount of blood," Trellis said.

"Amazing, isn't it?" Burton asked. "The human body only holds about nine pints, but spray just a

pint of that on a wall and it looks like a massacre."
He took one last photo, then set his camera down
outside the doorway. The bathroom had enough
spatter in it that setting anything down in the room
could disturb evidence. There was blood on the tiled
walls and floor, the sink, the toilet and the body of
Hank Roberts, who was slumped against the wall
across from the toilet.

"Is all of that blood from the deceased?" Trellis
asked.

"I think so, but the lab will find out for sure,"
Burton said.

"There does seem to be a difference in colouring,"
Trellis said. "We have dark red blood on Roberts's
head and face and the toilet tank lid over there," he
said, pointing to the broken ceramic slab, which lay
near the bowl, "with spatters of the same colour
going from the toilet to the body." He indicated the
path with his finger, and Burton nodded at the
maroon circles that led across the room.

"Then we have this bright red blood on the walls,
floor, and Roberts's face and chest," Trellis
continued, indicating the fine, elongated spatters.
"But there's no blood on the ceiling or the wall
opposite Roberts." Trellis mimicked holding the
toilet tank lid and striking Roberts in the head with
it several times. "If someone had killed him like this,
blood would have got on the toilet tank lid, and
when the killer swung the lid up, they would have
sprayed cast-off blood all over the place, including
the opposite wall and ceiling."

"Most likely," Burton said.

"Powder and brush, please," Trellis said, and Burton handed him the items from waistcoat pockets 22 and 16, respectively. Trellis dusted the toilet-tank lid but found nothing.

"So there aren't any fingerprints on the lid, and the blood on it shows that it hasn't been wiped." Trellis was starting to roll now, the sequence of possible events playing through his head quickly. "What injuries does Roberts have?" he asked.

"Preliminary examination shows a fractured skull and at least two broken ribs," Burton said. "X-rays will tell us if there are any other broken bones, but those were pretty apparent. You can see where—"

"Don't tell me!" Trellis yelled. He knew that if Burton got going, he would forget all about the unofficial test and rattle off his conclusions before Trellis could reach his own. "The assailant wore gloves," he said, "And only hit Roberts once. That's why there isn't any castoff on the ceiling and wall."

"If he only hit him once," Burton said, "where did all of this other spatter come from?" He pointed to the bright red specks on the wall, floor and Roberts. From their shape, Trellis could tell that the blood had hit the surfaces at a high speed.

"The attacker struck him with the tank lid once," Trellis said, knowing he was guessing, "then hit Roberts several times after that with his fists, or an object that he took with him."

Burton just pointed to the ceiling and opposite wall.

"I know, I know," Trellis said. "That would have caused castoff, too. OK, you win. What happened here?"

"What happened is," Burton said, "you didn't check the entire scene before speculating about what happened. Look on the other side of the toilet." Trellis had a moment of terror in which he imagined what he might find there. But when he did look, all he saw was a light bulb. He picked it up with gloved fingers and put it over his head.

"Aha!" he said. "The conclusion has arrived!"

How did Roberts die?

Trellis's File

Burton got me this time. He was right, I didn't check the scene thoroughly. Roberts was standing on his toilet, trying to replace the light bulb in the ceiling fixture and slipped. He hit his head on the toilet-tank lid, breaking it and his skull. His chest hit the toilet bowl, fracturing his ribs and puncturing his lung. The dark-red blood was from his head wound and it left a trail of drops to his body. The bright-red blood was due to his punctured lung. Oxygen-rich blood is always bright red, and it dripped from his nose and mouth every time he exhaled. Roberts didn't have an attacker, unless someone has worked out how to sue a toilet.

THE TOOTH OF THE
MATTER

Burton saw the Sensitive Cleaners van parked at the curb and pulled in behind it. Bug was talking to a woman in the front garden, and she seemed to be taking a half step away from him every five seconds or so. Burton approached them, bracing himself for what Bug had to say. But he was still shocked when he got within earshot.

"So the possum poops, they are not so soft," Bug was saying to the woman, who took another step away from him. "So they are easier to clean up. Raccoons, everhow, they leave such messes. I don't like raccoons."

"Hello, Mr Gorlach!" Burton called before the woman broke into a sprint.

"Ah, Burtons! You drive like syrup runs uphill!" Bug said by way of greeting. "We have been waiting for you for years!" He shook Burton's hand roughly then turned to the woman, who looked relieved to be finished with her conversation. Or so she thought.

"This is Mrs Krause," Bug said. "I am telling her about differences in animal droppings, since it is why she called me. She thought it was a squirrel who used her basement for a toilet, but it wasn't." Bug looked at Burton, waiting for the CSI to ask what kind of animal it was. This was all very exciting for Bug.

"So it wasn't a squirrel?" Burton asked. Bug shook his head, a sly smile creeping onto his face. His lips moved silently, as if they could barely hold back the answer.

"What kind of animal was it?" Burton said.

"Rats!" Bug hollered. "Big ones, too! Not like rats from back home, though. Those rats tip over cars and eat tyres. Mrs Krause's rats, they come into her basement through crack in foundation, have party, and leave. Not so terrible."

"I hope you didn't call me here because the rats invited you to the afterparty," Burton said, "and you need a date."

"No, no! Come with me, I will show," Bug said.

"I'll stay out here," Mrs Krause said. From the look she was giving her house, Burton wouldn't be surprised to find a removals van in the driveway by the time he returned. He followed Bug through the front door and into the basement, where the rat faeces were sitting along one wall.

"This is the biohazard," Bug said. "Rodents infest, and some could have the deadly hantavirus. We are safe, but don't kick dookie around or sniff it."

"I'll do my best," Burton said.

"This is why I call you, Burtons," Bug said and pointed near the crack in the concrete foundation. "Do you see it?"

There was dirt spilling onto the basement floor from the crack, and Burton assumed some of the soil had come from the rats. He leaned a bit closer and finally did see it: a tooth.

"The tooth? Is that what I'm looking for?" Burton asked as he snapped on a pair of gloves from waistcoat pocket 5.

"Yes, yes," said Bug. "Is it person?"

"Hard to tell right away," Burton said and took a few photos of the small off-white bone. "A lot of animal bones can look very similar to human. A front bear paw looks a lot like a human hand, and a rib cage from a deer can easily be mistaken for a person's. But we won't know for sure until we run the DNA or find the rest of the skeleton." He plucked the tooth out of the dirt and brushed it off, carefully turning it in his hands. A glint of silver caught his eye. He nodded and slipped it into an evidence bag from waistcoat pocket 9.

"You will have Ed sniff the ground to find the body?" Bug asked hopefully. Bug never tired of throwing the tennis ball for Ed, which made him one of her best friends.

"I don't have her with me today," Burton said as they made their way up the stairs. "But we can try a few other ways to find the burial spot." Outside the house, along the same wall as the foundation crack, Burton took a portable conductivity meter out of waistcoat pocket 28.

"What is this?" Bug asked when he saw the tool.

"It tests how well the soil conducts electricity," Burton said. "The higher the number it reads, the more conductive the soil is."

"This dirt is electrifying?" Bug said, eyeing the ground.

"It doesn't contain electricity, but the moisture in the soil allows electricity to pass through," said Burton. "So if the soil has a lot of moisture, it will give a higher reading on the meter. You wait here, this shouldn't take long." He started at one corner and made his way along the wall, taking a measurement of the ground every four feet. The measurements came back 2.0, 2.15, 2.1, 4.6, 2.3, 2.0, and 2.2.

Burton walked back to the spot that measured 4.6 and began to run his CRIME SEEN? tape. "Congratulations, Bug. You helped find a buried human being."

How did he know the skeleton was human, and how did he know where it was buried?

Burton's File

The flash of silver in the tooth was a filling, and only a human tooth would have that. The 4.6 reading on the conductivity meter indicated that the soil in that spot contained more moisture than the others. When a buried body decomposes, it adds moisture to the surrounding soil.

THE WALKING STIFF

"He was a zombie, I tell you! A zombie!"

Burton could hear the man in the interview room yelling from across the hall, and he looked at Mike Trellis for an explanation. The CSI technician was dressed in his usual Halloween costume, which consisted of him carrying around a cereal box with a knife stuck in it. A new administrative assistant walked by, and Trellis said "I'm a cereal killer. Get it?"

The woman kept walking.

"She's upset because my costume is better than hers," Trellis said to Burton.

"Right," said Burton. "What's this I hear about a zombie?"

"Oh, that guy," Trellis said, frowning towards the interview room. "It's Jim Lee, the new part-time morgue attendant. He's freaking out because he thinks he saw a dead guy walking around."

"Well, it is Halloween," Burton said. "The day

when the dead rise and walk the earth, and we have to dress like corpses to blend in with them."

"If that's the reason for Halloween, why are there so many clown costumes?" Trellis asked, his voice rising to a manic pitch.

"Because even the dead won't mess with clowns," Burton said as they made their way towards the interview room. Inside, Detective Frank Gibson was standing and shaking his head at Jim Lee, who was sitting with his face in his hands.

"It was awful! Just awful!" Lee said. "Now I have to find a new job! I can't possibly stay in a work environment that has the undead walking around."

"I don't know," Gibson said. "Seems like it would be nice and quiet. Except for all that shuffling that zombies do."

"Mr Lee," Burton said. "Can you take us through what happened? Hopefully, we can find a logical explanation for this incident."

"Incident?" Lee cried. "How about earth-shaking event! The dead have returned!"

"Right, we've got that part," said Burton. "But take us through it, just the same." Lee took a deep breath, sipped his water with a shaky hand and started talking.

"I was processing the paperwork for Warren Trudeau, who passed away last week. You probably remember him? You discovered evidence that he was murdered, but the killer hasn't been caught yet." Burton couldn't tell if that was a compliment or an insult, but he could see how Gibson took it by the detective's clenched jaw.

"I recall that case," Burton said. "There were signs of a struggle, but no trace of the assailant. There were two coffee cups on the table, and one of them had smudges that indicated fingerprints had been wiped off. But they both had Trudeau's DNA along the rim."

Gibson nodded. "We think the killer was looking for a winning lottery ticket Trudeau had. We found it hidden in his shoe during the autopsy. He must have told someone about it before he went to cash it in. We tried to contact his family to see if he told them, but the only person I've been able to track down is his brother – Dan, I think – and he hasn't called me back."

"Anyway," Lee said, "I put Trudeau in the cooler and filed his paperwork, then cleaned the area. About an hour later, I look up from my desk and see him walking around! I couldn't believe it! He was looking through drawers, opening cabinets, and when he finally got to my office, he looked in, saw me, and said 'Boo!'"

"The zombie said 'boo'?" Burton asked.

"I thought zombies just groaned," Gibson said. "You know: uuuuuuuuhhhhh."

"No," said Trellis. "Zombies say 'brains.' They just walk around going 'Brains … brains…'" Gibson and Trellis did their zombie impressions, shuffling into the corners and flapping their arms while Burton and Lee watched.

"All right," Burton said when it was over. "That was charming."

"So," Lee said, glancing at all three of them.

"Is there a plan for when zombies start to take over? Because I'm not really sure what to do."

"Yes, there is," said Burton. "We take fingerprints."

"That doesn't sound very helpful," Lee said.

"You said you cleaned before you saw the zombie," said Burton. "So the zombie's fingerprints will be the only ones on the drawers and cabinets, right?"

"I guess," Lee said. "I did a pretty thorough job."

"Mike," Burton said to Trellis. "Head down to the morgue and lift some prints off those surfaces, then meet me in the lab."

"What should I do?" Gibson asked.

"You can go back to doing your zombie impersonation," Burton said. "Or was that how you do your thinking? I've never seen either, so I don't know."

Less than an hour later, Trellis and Burton met in the lab. "Here are the zombie's prints," Trellis said. Burton placed one of them under one side of the comparison microscope, and put Trudeau's print under the other. He peered into the eyepieces, then stepped back and let Trellis have a look.

"They don't match," Trellis said. "So who is the zombie?"

"I'll give you a hint," Burton said. "He was there when Trudeau died, and he was there when he was born."

Who was the zombie?

The zombie was Warren Trudeau's identical twin, Dan. Warren told his brother about the winning lottery ticket and Dan tried to get it from him but ended up killing his twin in the process. Dan went to the morgue to sort through Warren's belongings in the hope that the ticket was there.

Identical twins have the same genotype, or DNA; that's why all the DNA at the crime scene appeared to belong to Warren. But they do not share the same phenotype, which determines such physical traits as fingerprints.

THE WISE DEDUCTION

Burton approached the ditch along the country road and spotted Detective Frank Gibson standing in the weeds alongside the culvert. The burly detective waved him over, a large paper cup of coffee in his hand and a sly grin on his face. Despite the chilly weather, Gibson seemed to be in fine spirits.

"I don't like the look of this at all," Burton muttered to himself. When he was within earshot, he found out why Gibson was so happy.

"Looks like they beat you to it," Gibson said, the smile spreading. He pointed to the yellow-and-black CRIME SCENE tape strung around an area of the ditch. "You won't be able to put up your cute 'crime seen?' tape today. What a shame."

Burton stopped next to the grinning detective. "I hope you didn't call me out here just for that," he said.

"No, no," Gibson reassured him, the smile gone. "Obviously we detectives and uniformed cops can't figure out what happened here, so we had to call the mighty Wes Burton to hold our hands." Gibson sniffed the cup of coffee he was holding. "Wait a minute! This smells like coffee! I think the killer drinks coffee!" He held the cup at arm's length and squinted at it. "Hold on, I think I brought this coffee with me. But I'm just a detective, so I can't tell for sure. Burton, will you check the cup for my fingerprints?"

While Burton waited patiently for Gibson to finish his rant, he checked his watch twice, popped a piece of gum in his mouth and retied his shoe. When the detective had finished jabbering, Burton gave him a flat look.

"What's the situation?" Burton asked.

Gibson took a sip of his coffee, smacked his lips a few times and finally decided to let Burton in on the details.

"A farmer found a skeleton in the ditch. We think it might be Nate Robertson, that 16-year-old who went missing last year."

"And he's been here the whole time?" Burton asked. "This isn't exactly a main road, but I'm sure someone has been down here in the past year."

"The farmer says this ditch has a few feet of water in it during the spring and most of the summer," Gibson said. "And with the sudden snow we had last autumn, I'm not surprised no one spotted the body. I didn't take a really close look, but it looks like a gunshot to the head was the checkmate on this one."

Burton eased down the slope into the ditch, careful to keep some distance from the skeleton. If any bones had detached and relocated, he didn't want to disturb them. The skeleton was lying face up, with the skull tilted a bit to the left. He was happy to see that the teeth were intact; maybe they could identify the body with dental records. For both the upper and lower sets of teeth, he counted four incisors, two canines, two pairs of premolars and three pairs of molars, taking close-up photos the entire time. He looked at the hole in the skull just above where the right ear would have been, and shined his torch into it.

"I see the hole," he said to Gibson. "It does look like a bullet entrance, and I don't see an exit yet, so hopefully the slug is still in the skull."

"I also noticed some scratches and scrapes on the skull," Gibson said. "Looks like whoever it was took a beating, either before or after the shooting."

Burton shook his head. "Those are most likely post-mortem and not from the killer," he said. Gibson looked confused.

"Animals," Burton explained. "Most likely rats and coyotes. Their teeth and claws scratched the skull when they were trying to get their meal off of it." Gibson looked at his coffee and set it down, suddenly no longer interested in any type of food. Burton smiled.

"We can confirm with dental records," he said. "But I can tell you right now this isn't the body of Nate Robertson."

How did Burton know?

Burton's File

The skeleton's teeth included three pairs of molars on both the upper and lower sets. The third pair of molars, sometimes referred to as wisdom teeth, typically don't appear until the age of 17 to 25. The skeleton had fully developed wisdom teeth, indicating that it could not be 16-year-old Nate Robertson.

TOO MUCH BILLIARDS ON THE BRAIN

Dr Crown began to gently pull the top of Gary Wolfe's skull off, then stopped. Burton and Trellis were looking on with a mixture of anticipation and apprehension. Crown looked at them, then let go of the skull, leaving it in place for the time being.

"What is it?" Burton asked. Spatter a brain on a wall, and he could tell you where it came from, what put it there and how fast it arrived. But leave it in the skull, and he was a bit lost.

"I want to give Michael a quick lesson in brain damage," Crown said.

"Isn't that kind of like giving a fish a lecture on being wet?" Burton asked.

"Ha-ha," Trellis said. "You want a real joke? Can I at least see the brain first, if you don't mind?" Trellis asked. "Get it… Brain … mind?" Crown shook her head.

"What would be the point if you don't know what

you're looking for?" she said, already entering instructor mode. "When there is an injury to the head, two kinds of trauma typically occur: coup and countercoup. Coup takes place at the point of impact, or where the brain was struck. Countercoup is directly opposite that point, on the other side of the head."

Crown picked up a container of waterless hand sanitizer, the clear plastic showing the thick substance inside. "Think of this container as your skull, and the fluid inside as your brain. As you can see, when I strike the side of the skull with a moving object, the brain is damaged at the point of impact and pulls away from the skull." Crown karate-chopped the side of the container, and Burton and Trellis watched the contents fly away from the side of the strike.

"However," Crown said. "If the skull is the moving object, such as when someone falls and hits their head on the ground, the most trauma occurs opposite the impact point." She held the container upright, then swung it 90 degrees and slapped it into the palm of her hand, stopping the movement abruptly. The contents pulled away from the side opposite her hand, leaving a few bubbles behind. Trellis imagined his brain sloshing around in his head like that and shivered.

"All right, then," Crown said, squirting a bit of the sanitizer onto her hands. "Tell me what you know about the case."

Trellis immediately referred to his notes, eager to look away from Dr Crown as she smeared the "brains" over her hands. "Our examination of the body showed cause of death to be a fracture at the back of the skull, with a blue powdery substance in the hair."

Crown nodded at this and motioned for Trellis to continue. "The witness report states that Wolfe was playing 9-ball billiards with some friends in his garage. He was sitting down and leaning back in his chair, and he tipped over backward and cracked his head on the floor. His friends tried to revive him and called an ambulance, but he was pronounced dead before he reached the hospital." Trellis showed Crown some photos of the crime scene. They included a shot of the billiard table, with nine balls spread out across the green felt.

"Whoever shot first didn't do very well," he said. "They didn't get any balls in the pockets. That's all I have. Should we look at the brain now?"

"I think the time has come," Crown said. She stepped forwards and eased the top of Wolfe's skull off, exposing the grey matter underneath. She gave a small nod, as if what she saw confirmed what she already suspected.

"There is substantial haemorrhaging around the occipital lobe," Crown said, indicating the rear of the brain. Trellis leaned in for a better look, a grimace on his face.

Burton did not look, because he was busy examining the photos of the billiard table. He counted nine balls, and the report stated that the group had indeed been playing 9-ball. The billiard balls were lying so that he could see at least a partial amount of the number on each.

"Hey, boss," Trellis said to Burton. "You want to take a look at this? We think maybe Wolfe didn't die from his head hitting the ground."

"I know he didn't," Burton said. "And I have a description of the killer. It's white, round and missing from this billiard table."

How did Wolfe die?

Crown's explanation of coup versus countercoup indicates that Wolfe died from the impact of a moving object to the back of his skull. If he had hit his head on the ground like witnesses claimed, the internal bleeding would have been at the front of the brain, not the rear.

Wolfe and his friends were playing 9-ball, and there were nine balls on the table, but there should have been a tenth: the cue ball. The blue powder around Wolfe's fracture suggests cue chalk, which rubbed off of the cue stick, onto the ball, and onto Wolfe's head when the cue ball struck him.

THE STINKY CEILING STAIN

Burton and Mike Trellis followed the vacuum hose from the Sensitive Cleaners van into the apartment building, up two flights of stairs and through an open apartment door. Inside, Bug was standing with a man and a woman, all three of them looking up at the ceiling.

"What's up?" Trellis said. "Get it? Because you're looking up."

"Bah-ha-ha!" Bug laughed, bending over and holding on to the woman to keep from falling over. He laughed for almost a minute before he could speak. "Ah, Mikes, your words are like laughing gas, only not flammable."

"Thanks, Bug," Trellis said and looked at Burton. "See? He thinks I'm funny."

"He also makes money cleaning up rat poop," Burton said. "I think his tastes might be a little unique." Burton turned to Bug. "What's the story here?"

"Ah, Burtons," Bug said. "I am called here by Stans and Katherines to clean up a stain on their ceiling. When I see it and then smell it, I know right away you should take looks before I do anything." Stan and Katherine looked confused, but they nodded anyway.

"Thanks for thinking of me," Burton said. He looked up at the stain on the ceiling. "Mostly brown, but I see some dark red here and there. And you're right, Bug, it smells bad. Stan, Katherine, do you know who lives in the apartment above you?"

"That's Mr Walton," Katherine said. "But we haven't seen him for a few days. You don't think he … died, do you?"

"Maybe we should go upstairs and see what Mr Walton has to say about it," Burton said. "Mike, can you call the apartment manager and ask him to meet us upstairs with a key?"

"You got it," Trellis said, and started dialling.

"Is big mess," Bug said to no one in particular. "When body decays, it leaks all over floor. Sometimes bursts, you know, pop!"

Stan looked like he might faint, and Katherine started covering the furniture and carpet with bin bags in case the stain decided to spread.

"Bug," Burton said, "why don't you come upstairs with us?"

"Ah, yes, good," Bug said. "Stans, Katherines, do you want to come, too?"

Burton didn't think it was possible, but Stan and Katherine both got paler. They didn't know what to say.

"They'd better stay here," Burton said. "If it is a

crime scene, we can't have any unauthorized personnel." Bug nodded, happy that he was authorized.

Burton, Trellis and Bug went upstairs and met the apartment manager at Mr Walton's door.

"Who has to pay for this if the guy died and left a mess?" the manager said.

"I'm sure your insurance will cover it," Burton said. "But we don't know that anyone died, so please open the door."

The manager unlocked the door and stepped back.

Mr Walton's body was lying face up in the middle of the living room. The smell inside was much worse, and Burton pulled three filter masks out of waistcoat pocket 13. He handed one to Trellis and one to Bug, but Bug already had his own. It was better than the ones Burton had, with two filters instead of one. And it looked cooler, with black rubber and chrome fasteners.

"Do you have any more of those?" Trellis asked him.

"No, sorry," said Bug. His mask made him sound like a robot. Trellis shrugged and put on the mask Burton gave him, but he wasn't happy about it.

Burton figured out quickly why the room smelled so bad.

"That's a very large humidifier over there," he said, pointing to a large device against the wall that was still humming. "And the temperature has to be around 85. With the high heat and humidity, Mr Walton has been decaying at a very rapid rate. Bug, please stand here by the door while Mike and I check the body."

"But I am authorized," Bug said.

"Right," said Burton. "I need you to make sure no unauthorized people get in."

"Just let them try," Bug said, pulling a can of industrial cleaner out of his belt pouch. He stood in the doorway facing out, giving a suspicious look to the manager and everything else in the hallway.

"I wish we could bring him to every scene," Burton said. He and Trellis approached Mr Walton's body, careful not to step in any of the fluids that had spread across the floor. The skin had started to change from dark purple to greenish-black, except for pale spots on the forehead, left cheek and jaw. There was almost no blood beneath these spots.

"How long do you think he's been here?" Trellis said.

"Could be only a few days, with the climate in here," said Burton.

Trellis said, "Stan and Katherine are not going to be happy when they find out what that stain on their ceiling is."

"That's nothing," said Burton. "Wait until they discover that someone knew he was dead and didn't tell anyone."

How did Burton know?

Burton's File

When a body dies, the blood stops moving through the blood vessels. Gravity pulls the blood to the lowest areas of the body and creates a purplish discoloration called lividity. However, any part of the body that presses against a surface, such as the floor, remains pale because the weight of the body prevents the blood from settling there.

The pale spots on Mr Walton's face indicate that he died face down, and lividity set in while his face was pressed against the floor. Someone found him that way and rolled him onto his back but didn't inform the authorities.

GLOSSARY

Accelerant A flammable material used to start a fire.

Autopsy The examination of a corpse to determine or confirm the cause of death.

Blood spatter The pattern of blood deposits at a crime scene that can help determine what occurred at the scene.

Convict (noun) A person found guilty of an offence or crime.

(verb) To prove someone guilty of a crime in court.

Deceased A body that is no longer living.

Decompose When a body starts to decay or break down after death.

DNA The molecule that carries the genetic information in the cell. Traces of DNA from saliva, skin, blood and other sources can be used to identify the person who left the trace.

EMT Emergency medical technician.

Evidence Any physical item that assists in proving or disproving a conclusion. For example, a paint scraping is evidence; an eyewitness account is not.

Homicide The killing of one person by another.

Lividity The discoloration of the skin caused by the settling of blood that occurs in a body after the heart stops.

Postmortem Occurring after death.

Trace element A very small bit of chemicals or evidence.

UV light Ultraviolet light, also known as black light, is used to identify many trace evidence items such as body fluids, drugs and inks.